LIFE CYCLE OF A COW

by Noah Leatherland

Minneapolis, Minnesota

Credits

All images are courtesy of Shutterstock.com, unless otherwise specified. With thanks to Getty Images, Thinkstock Photo, and iStockphoto. Cover – tanyaya, Fancy Tapis, YummyBuum, BigMouse, Eric Isselee. Recurring images – nikiteev_konstantin, uiliaaa, YummyBuum, Terdpong, tanyaya. 2 – Clara Bastian, Eric Isselee. 4 – Zurijeta, Krakenimages.com, Paul Hakimata Photography. 5 – Fotoluminate LLC, Ebtikar, Dernkadel. 6 – tbradford. 7 – VanderWolf Images. 8 – Pablo Debat. 9 – Ksjundra07. 10 – Nektarstock. 11 – Kath Watson. 12 – Adam Gryko. 13 – Zacchio. 14 – Clara Bastian. 15 – ehasdemir. 16 – Show Business, Birgitta Kullman. 17 – rghenry. 18 – Eric Isselee. 19 – alberto clemares exposito. 20 – 135pixels. 21 – OlgaLucky. 22 – Eric Isselee, DmytroPerov. 23 – Irina Kozorog.

Library of Congress Cataloging-in-Publication Data is available at www.loc.gov or upon request from the publisher.

ISBN: 979-8-88916-959-8 (hardcover)
ISBN: 979-8-89232-487-8 (paperback)
ISBN: 979-8-89232-123-5 (ebook)

© 2025 BookLife Publishing
This edition is published by arrangement with BookLife Publishing.

North American adaptations © 2025 Bearport Publishing Company. All rights reserved. No part of this publication may be reproduced in whole or in part, stored in any retrieval system, or transmitted in any form or by any means, electronic, mechanical, photocopying, recording, or otherwise, without written permission from the publisher. Bearport Publishing is a division of Chrysalis Education Group.

For more information, write to Bearport Publishing, 5357 Penn Avenue South, Minneapolis, MN 55419.

Contents

What Is a Life Cycle?........4
Cows on the Farm...........6
Getting Ready for Calves.....8
Cute Calves...............10
Mother's Milk.............12
Growing Up Fast..........14
Name That Cow!..........16
All Grown Up.............18
The End of Life...........20
Life Cycle of a Cow........22
Glossary..................24
Index....................24

WHAT IS A LIFE CYCLE?

All living things go through different stages of life. We come into the world and grow over time. Eventually, we die. This is the life cycle.

BABY

TODDLER

CHILD

As humans, we start life as babies. We grow into toddlers and children. Then, we become teenagers. Finally, we are adults and get even older. We may have babies of our own, and then the cycle begins again.

COWS ON THE FARM

Animals on the farm go through life cycles, too. Farm cows are **domestic** animals. This means they are not wild. People keep them as **livestock**.

Cows that farmers raise for their milk are called dairy cows.

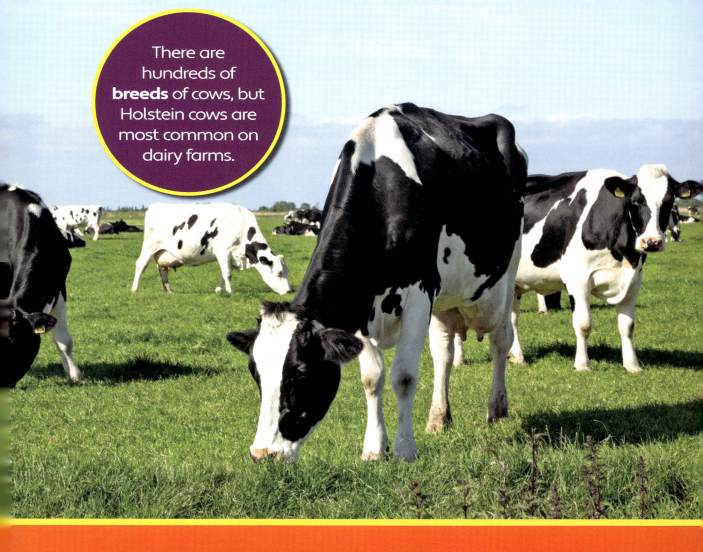

There are hundreds of **breeds** of cows, but Holstein cows are most common on dairy farms.

A group of cows is called a herd. Some farms have only a few cows, while others have hundreds or thousands. Farmers raise these animals for their meat and for their milk.

GETTING READY FOR CALVES

Female cows can have babies called calves. Usually, a **pregnant** cow has only one calf growing inside her at a time. After about nine months, the baby is ready to be born.

A PREGNANT COW

A female cow that has not yet had a baby is called a heifer (HEF-ur).

When it is time to give **birth**, the mother cow finds a safe place to be alone. Sometimes, she gives birth by herself. Other times, farmers may need to help get her calf out.

CUTE CALVES

When a calf is born, its mother licks it all over. This cleans the calf and helps the mother and baby **bond**. The newborn calf will be able to stand and walk soon after.

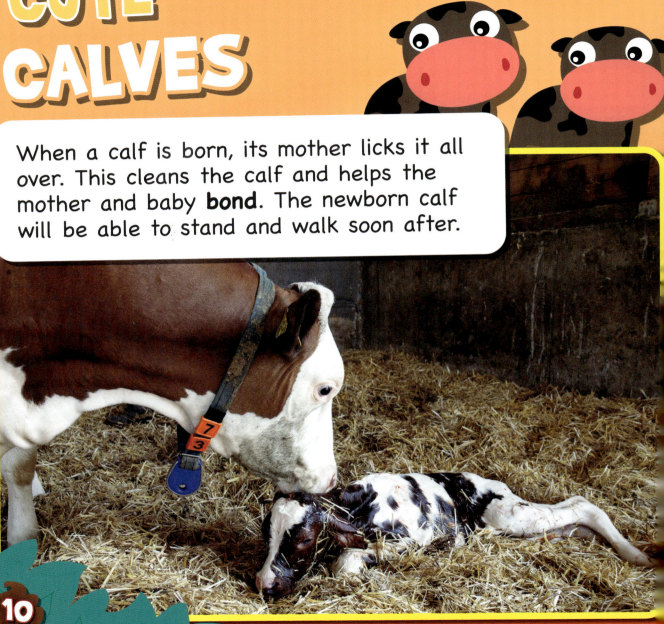

Most newborn calves are about the same height as a large dog.

Newborn calves can be very large. Many kinds of dairy calves weigh about 90 pounds (40 kg) when they are born.

MOTHER'S MILK

It is important for a calf to drink milk from its mother within two hours of being born. This milk gives the calf the **nutrients** it needs to have a healthy start to life.

The mother cow makes milk in a part of her body called an udder.

AN UDDER

A mother cow's body makes milk for about 10 months after her calf is born. Often, there is more milk than her calf needs. Farmers take the extra milk from the mother during this time.

GROWING UP FAST

Calves grow quickly by drinking their mother's milk. They may munch on some hay, too. After a few months, the calves eat only solid food.

Cows and older calves eat mostly grasses and grains.

Calves are sometimes kept separate from adults until they are bigger.

Dairy calves weigh about 400 lb. (180 kg) when they are 6 months old. By 1 year, they may weigh more than 660 lb. (300 kg). That's almost the same weight as a motorcycle.

NAME THAT COW!

When calves are about a year old, they look like smaller adult cows. However, they are still growing! This is like the teenager stage for humans. **Males**, called bull calves, are bigger and grow faster than heifer female calves.

A HEIFER CALF

A BULL CALF

Calves that are about a year old may be called feeders or growers. This is because they spend their days eating grass in fields on the farms.

ALL GROWN UP

Cows are considered fully grown when they are about two years old. A heifer usually has her first calf at about this time, too. Then, she is just called a cow.

Many breeds of cows have horns. Usually, the males have larger horns than the females.

Fully grown males are usually much larger than females. They can weigh up to 4,000 lb. (1,800 kg). These big bulls are often kept in fields away from the rest of the herd.

THE END OF LIFE

Cows that live on farms don't have many **predators**. However, they can become sick. Farmers need to make sure their cows have clean food and water, as well as regular checkups to keep them healthy.

Veterinarians are people who take care of the health of animals.

A cow can live for about 20 years. However, farm cows raised for their meat usually don't live this long.

LIFE CYCLE OF A COW

A cow begins life as a calf. Its mother licks the baby cow clean, and it quickly learns to walk. The calf drinks its mother's milk and grows bigger. Eventually, it becomes an adult.

CALF

ADULT COW

During its life, a cow may give birth to calves of its own. Eventually, the cow will die, but the calves live on and have even more cows. This keeps the life cycle going!

Glossary

birth when a female has a baby

bond to form a close relationship

breeds different types of an animal

domestic tamed for use by humans

female a cow that can give birth to young

livestock animals that are raised by people on farms or ranches

males cows that cannot give birth to young

nutrients substances needed by plants and animals to grow and stay healthy

predators animals that hunt and eat other animals

pregnant when a female animal has a baby growing inside her

Index

birth 9, 23
breeds 7, 19
bull 16
calves 8, 10–18, 22–23
domestic 6
farmers 6–7, 9, 13, 20
food 14, 20
heifer 8, 16, 18
horns 19
milk 6–7, 12–14, 22
predators 20